Flexible Thinking

Program

By
Melissa Mullin, Ph.D

www.KandMCenter.com

Copyright ©2012 The K&M Center, Inc.

ABOUT THE AUTHOR

MELISSA MULLIN fell in love with teaching while designing educational computer games for The Walt Disney Educational Media Company. Pursuing that interest, she received a Ph.D. in Educational Psychology, with a specialization in Learning and instruction from UCLA. Enjoying the challenge of helping students at all levels learn, she opened the K&M Center, a learning center in Santa Monica, CA with Karen Fried, Psy.D. As creators of the K&M Center, Karen and Melissa set themselves a mission to help every student learn to his or her potential. Melissa and Karen work with parents, teachers, tutors and other professionals to individualize a truly effective program for each child. After over 18 years of helping thousands of children learn to read, write and achieve in school Melissa is now using the knowledge she has gained to create products that can guide teachers and parents who wish to help children learn. In her blog, www.bitsofwisdomforall.com, Melissa shares the insights she gathers as she works with her students and their families. In addition to teaching, Melissa enjoys spending time with her family reading, biking and skiing.

Learn more about Melissa
and other K&M products at
www.kandmcenter.com

Special Appreciation

to our staff in helping us develop and test these materials:

Katie Sibley

Michele LaFemina

Designed by:
Meredith Noel

www.KandMCenter.com

Copyright ©2012 The K&M Center, Inc.

Flexible Thinking Program

Table of Contents

- **Introduction** .... page 2

- **Administering the Flexible Thinking Program** 3
  - Keeping Students in "The Zone"
  - Metacognition

- **Explaining the Flexible Thinking Program to Students** 7

- **Student Contract** 8

- **Activities Summaries** 9

- **Progress Charts** 12
  - SAMPLE Progress Chart
  - Progress Charts

- **Strategy Recording Sheet** 15

- **Activities Directions and Worksheets**
  1. Crossing the Midline
     - Infinity Signs 16
     - Simon Says 25
     - Hand Tasks 28
  2. Changing the Rules
     - Color Shift 29
     - Direction Shift 31
     - Shape Shift 34
     - Sorting 36
     - The Set Game 40
  3. Organizing Your Thoughts
     - Describe and Draw 41
     - Tower of Hanoi 49
  4. Different Ways to the Same Answer
     - Optical Illusions 50
     - Mapping 57
  5. Stop-ability
     - The Telephone Game 63
     - Spot It 68

- **Additional Resources and Games to Support Flexible Thinking** 69

www.KandMCenter.com

Copyright ©2012 The K&M Center, Inc.

Flexible Thinking Program

Introduction

Flexible thinking means you are able to find more than one way to do something. Sometimes it means being able to change your plan in response to a change that occurs. Other times it means adapting to a friend or teacher's way of doing things. Yet other times, it means adjusting to a new routine.

Flexible thinking allows you to bend and adjust both your body and your mind. The willow tree can survive when other trees don't because it can bend in the wind rather than break. Learning how to bend when you are faced with new ideas or ways of doing something helps you adjust and do well.

Flexible thinkers are able to "let go" and allow for changes in their plan or idea to be made. For example, if a student thought the color of the dress in the story was red, can s/he look back and change her/his mental image of the dress from red to blue? Flexible thinkers **can** let go of their first thought to allow a correction to be made.

To build flexible thinking skills, we have compiled a variety of games and activities that encourage set shifting (letting go of one idea to consider another). Playing these games requires coaching to build and develop flexible thinking skills. Ask thought provoking questions to help your child find the answer and encourage her/him to try out all different types of strategies together in a safe no-stakes environment.

The key to the program is guided problem-solving through (sometimes) difficult tasks. Flexible thinking, like physical flexibility, requires stretching and constant adaptation as skills are developed. Each and every session, the student will be challenged to stretch a little bit further, consistently developing and adding strategies to their problem solving "toolbox." As such, this program is designed to grow with your student as s/he becomes a more flexible thinker.

www.KandMCenter.com

Copyright ©2012 The K&M Center, Inc.

Administering the Flexible Thinking Program

This program is meant to cultivate flexible thinking skills through consistent, supported practice over a span of forty-eight sessions. Repeated practice of these activities ultimately opens up previously blocked or unused pathways in the brain.

Length of the Program:
- 30 minute sessions
- 4 sessions a week
- 48 sessions total

Each Session:
- Student does a variety of 3-10 flexible thinking activities (selected by student and/or instructor)
- Track activities on Progress Chart
- Do prior to homework
- Encourage overlap of thinking skills and strategies into homework

It is important that your student be monitored throughout the program for two main reasons: to ensure they're kept in their **ZPD** and to ask guiding **METACOGNITIVE QUESTIONS**.

1. Staying in the Zone (ZPD)

First, you want to make sure your student is being kept in what psychologist Lev Vygotsky called the Zone of Proximal Development (ZPD). The ZPD is the space between what the learner has already mastered and what he or she can achieve when provided with educational support. In other words, the ZPD is the gap between what a student can do completely on their own (current ability level) and what they need support to do (ability beyond reach). When in their ZPD, students are challenged enough to remain engaged, yet not so challenged that they are overwhelmed by the task.

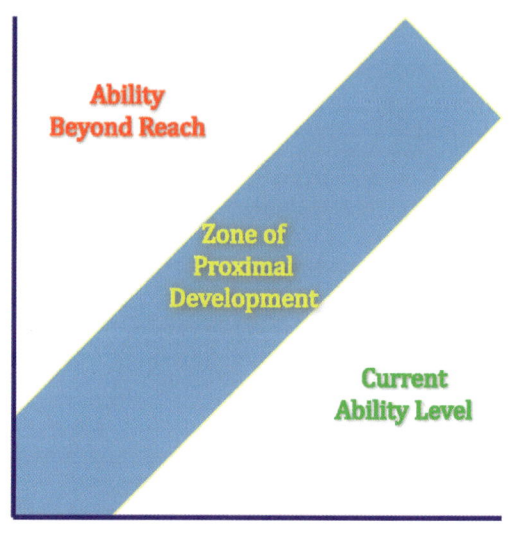

The Zone of Proximal Development

www.KandMCenter.com

Copyright ©2012 The K&M Center, Inc.

ADMINISTERING THE FLEXIBLE THINKING PROGRAM

By guiding a learner through specific tasks that may be above his/her independent level, the instructor can emphasize connections to what the student already knows in order to help the student gain independence. By asking METACOGNITIVE QUESTIONS and catering to an individual's learning style, this program allows the instructor to find a balance between what has already been achieved and the potential for achievement by providing support until the learner is ready to move through the task independently.

To help guide students through the program and to keep them in their ZPD, monitoring using the Flexible Thinking Progress Charts is important. The instructor and the student can confer on how easily the task was completed. Using colored markers, pencils, or crayons - the boxes on the chart are filled in:

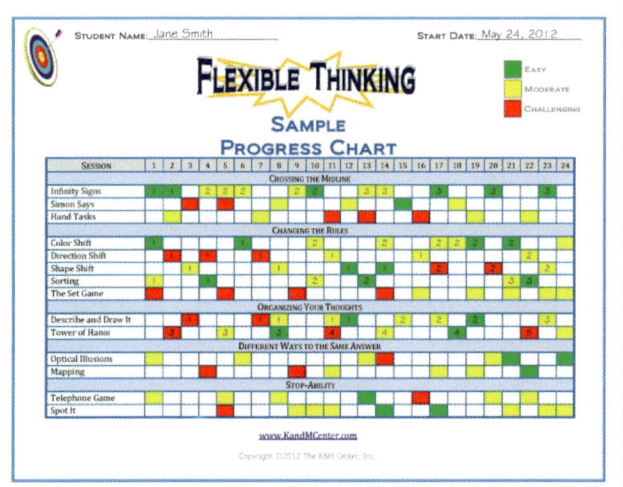

- RED if the activity was CHALLENGING *(above the ZPD)* for the student.

- YELLOW if the task was MODERATE *(in the ZPD)* for the student.

- GREEN if the task was EASY *(below the ZPD)* for the student.

Once a student is consistently in green with a task, it's time to make it more challenging.

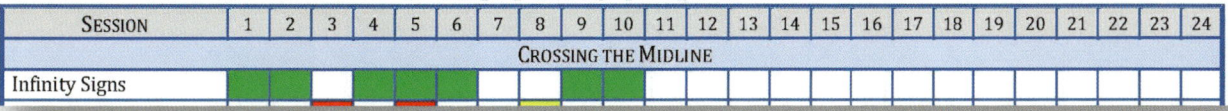

Conversely, if a student is staying consistent with reds in a task, it might be necessary to make some modifications.

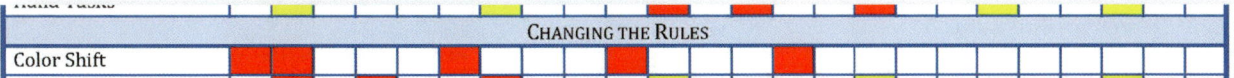

It is also helpful, for some activities, to note in the Progress Chart what level/rule the student completed in the session. For example, if the student is doing 3 rings on the Tower of Hanoi with ease, you could note a 3 in the box that you also color green. What will most likely happen next is a couple of sessions at 4 rings with yellow coloring. The hope is that after a few sessions, 4 rings would become a green box. Then, it would be time to move to 5 rings. Noting these numbers in these boxes will help you keep track of where your student is in the program.

www.KandMCenter.com

Copyright ©2012 The K&M Center, Inc.

2. Metacognitive Questioning

Metacognitive questioning throughout the program is the second instructor-integral component. Teaching student's metacognition, or "thinking about thinking" helps them take control of their learning process. At first, the instructor will be instrumental in guiding the student through the questions. However, the goal is for the student to internalize these questions and to be able to self-monitor on their own by the end of the program. These metacognitive questions should be carried over to homework time. Some examples of metacognitive questions students should be asking themselves throughout the activities and homework are noted below (note that not all questions fit all activities):

BEFORE THE TASK, when planning, students should get in the habit of thinking about:

- How much time do I have to complete this task?
- Why am I doing this?
- What do I already know that will help me with this?
- What do I want this to look like when it's done?
- What should I do first? second? third?
- What strategies will I use to help me complete this task?

DURING THE TASK, while the student is monitoring their plan of action, they should get in the habit of thinking:

- How am I doing?
- Am I on the right track?
- How should I proceed?
- Am I heading toward my goal?
- Am I spending the right amount of time on this?
- What do I need to do if I get stuck?
- What do I need to do if I don't understand?
- How will I know when I'm done?
- What strategies am I using?

www.KandMCenter.com

Copyright ©2012 The K&M Center, Inc.

ADMINISTERING THE FLEXIBLE THINKING PROGRAM

AFTER THE TASK, when the student is evaluating their plan of action, they should be asking themselves:

- Did I produce more or less than I had expected?
- Is the outcome better or worse than I anticipated?
- Was the process easier or more difficult than I thought it would be? Why?
- What strategies were the most helpful?
- What could I have done differently?
- Do I need to go back through the task and fill in any "blanks?"

The nature of guiding a student out of their comfort zone may cause some anxiety and frustration. The question is: how do you help when this anxiety and frustration arise? This is where metacognitive conversations become critical. Students who have significant strengths along with significant weaknesses are always going to have areas that trip them up.

In order for these students to feel secure, they need a stable cognitive baseline that they understand. This is what Mel Levine describes as "the demystifying process." The demystification process means taking the mystery out of how the brain works. The process requires you to shine a light on the child's strengths and weaknesses. By doing so, you will be able to take away the mystery of why some tasks are much more difficult than others. The important factor in all of this is developing a plan that doesn't act as a Band-Aid for areas of weakness. The solution requires developing a plan that remediates, or builds the areas of weakness so there is no longer a significant difference between the strengths and weaknesses. The goal is to keep the student in their ZPD, engaged, and challenged yet not pushed beyond their current capability.

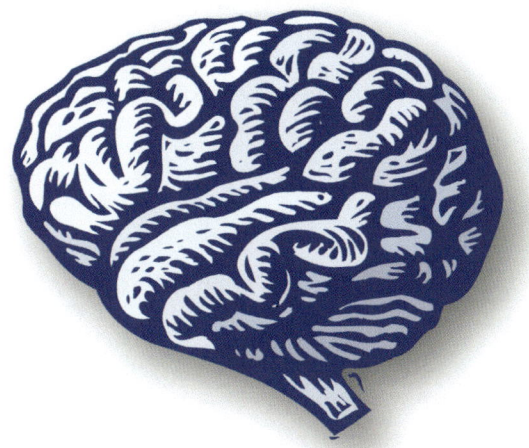

Your child will stretch their brain in ways that are crucial for success as a student!

www.KandMCenter.com

Copyright ©2012 The K&M Center, Inc.

EXPLAINING FLEXIBLE THINKING TO STUDENTS

It is important for students to understand how the work they'll be doing in the Flexible Thinking Program will help them in tangible ways, so you'll want to have a discussion with them as you begin about what Flexible Thinking is and why they're doing it.

Here are some guiding questions that you and your student can discuss:

- What does it mean to have a flexible body? *(can stretch, bend, etc…)*

- Who are people who rely on having flexible bodies? *(gymnasts, yoga teachers, runners, etc…)*

- How do they practice and get more flexible? *(keep stretching, slowly go beyond what they could previously do, practice, etc…)*

- What does it mean to have a flexible mind? *(can problem-solve, can find different ways to do things, can "go with the flow")*

- What things do you think require mental flexibility? *(puzzles, friendships, etc…)*

- What subjects in school do you think require mental flexibility? Give examples in each subject. *(Math – being able to do a problem more than 1 way, Reading – adjusting your mental picture of a character you're reading about based on new information, Writing – varying your sentence structure, History – taking a different side than what you personally agree with on a debate, Science – disproving a hypothesis)*

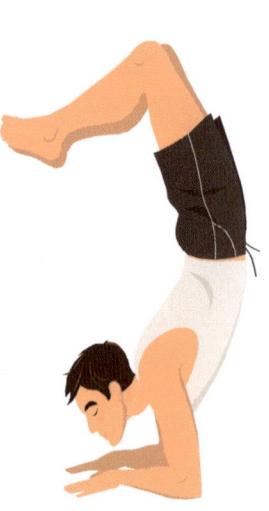

A great, concrete example of Flexible Thinking can be found in the story "Mirta the Super Fly," which is available as a free, downloadable app in iTunes:
https://itunes.apple.com/us/app/mirta-super-fly-brainy-fables/id513029515?mt=8

Discuss:
- What was Mirta lacking?

Be sure to click on the Author's Notes section. There it will explain Flexible Thinking and how it could have benefitted Mirta the Super Fly.

Tell students that though each Flexible Thinking activity is a game that may seem un-related to academics, together you will be working on developing strategies that WILL carry over to their schoolwork. You will work together to come up with strategies that should be recorded, either on the provided Strategy Recording Sheet or on Flashcards for reference.

www.KandMCenter.com

Copyright ©2012 The K&M Center, Inc.

Student & Parent Contract

Dear Parent,

To ensure the success of this program we need your assistance. We will provide the structure and organization that we want your child to learn; however, we depend on you to ensure that your child completes the work. To improve your child's Flexible Thinking, we have designed a Progress Chart for your child. We ask you to complete the Progress Chart together to ensure that progress is being made.

We have included a contract for you and your student to sign, signifying your willingness to work as a team to help your student improve his/her Flexible Thinking skills.

— THE CONTRACT —

I, _____, agree to complete the Flexible Thinking activities assigned to me.

I, _____, agree to work with my student to help him/her achieve his/her Flexible Thinking goals.

We, _____ and _____, agree that building Flexible Thinking skills is valuable. We will help each other remember our agreement.

What is the best way to communicate to send suggestions and get updates?

Email: _____

Phone: _____

www.KandMCenter.com

Copyright ©2012 The K&M Center, Inc.

Flexible Thinking Program

Activities Summaries

We have carefully compiled fifteen activities that require and build flexible thinking skills. The activities are separated into five sections:

1. **Crossing the Midline**
2. **Changing the Rules**
3. **Organizing Your Thoughts**
4. **Different Ways to the Same Answer**
5. **Stop-a-bility**

Each section of activities encourages flexible thinking in a different way. Practiced, in conjunction, they comprise a well-balanced plan to build flexible thinking skills.

While flexible thinking can be practiced with games, flexible thinking itself is critical for many academic tasks. So with each section is listed the academic importance of that skill.

Crossing the Midline Activities–
for Reading (left-to-right fluency),
Handwriting (fine motor),
Body Movements (gross motor).

CROSSING THE MIDLINE activities *encourage students to use both sides of his/her brain together. They generally involve physically crossing over the "midline," an invisible line down the center of the body that separates the body into "left side" and "right side." Crosses can happen with hands, arms, feet, and legs (e.g. "put your right hand on your left shoulder"). Practice in this area helps build the ability to coordinate one side of the brain with the other.*

- **INFINITY SIGNS** – students cross their mid-line by tracing, writing, then air-writing different sized infinity signs.

- **SIMON SAYS** – students do a variety of physical movements that require concentration and mental flexibility.

- **HAND TASKS** – students do a variety of movements with their left and right hands doing the same, than different things.

www.KandMCenter.com

Copyright ©2012 The K&M Center, Inc.

ACTIVITIES SUMMARIES

CHANGING THE RULES ACTIVITIES-
for Reading and Math.

CHANGING THE RULES activities *are classic examples of set shifting. The student is asked to do a task then they must shift to doing it a new or different way. Successful learners are able to quickly and seamlessly shift their thoughts in novel ways.*

- **COLOR SHIFT** – students look at a sheet of words that name colors and follow the leveled directions as to how to "read" the words.

- **DIRECTION SHIFT** – students look at a sheet of colored arrows and follow the leveled directions as to how to "read" the arrows.

- **SHAPE SHIFT** – students look at a sheet of shapes and follow the leveled directions as to how to "read" the shapes.

- **SORTING** – students sort a deck of 6 cards based on a variety of different characteristics.

- **THE SET GAME** – card game where students make "sets" (3 cards that are either all alike or all different in each attribute)

ORGANIZING YOUR THOUGHTS ACTIVITIES-
for Writing and Math.

ORGANIZING YOUR THOUGHTS activities *encourage students to stop, think, and organize their thoughts before they execute their plan. For example, they may want to "zoom out" and think about the big picture before they start going into details.*

- **DESCRIBE AND DRAW** – leveled activity where students chose a picture to accurately and effectively describe to another person using only their words. The other person draws what the student describes.

- **TOWER OF HANOI** – puzzle game where the student is challenged to move disks strategically from one pole to another.

www.KandMCenter.com

Copyright ©2012 The K&M Center, Inc.

ACTIVITIES SUMMARIES

DIFFERENT ROUTES TO THE SAME ANSWERS ACTIVITIES-
for Math, Reading, Problem-Solving, and Social Skills.

DIFFERENT ROUTES TO THE SAME ANSWERS activities *help students see that for many problems, there is not just one way to look at it or do it. These activities help the student open up to the possibility of taking different approaches to problem-solving.*

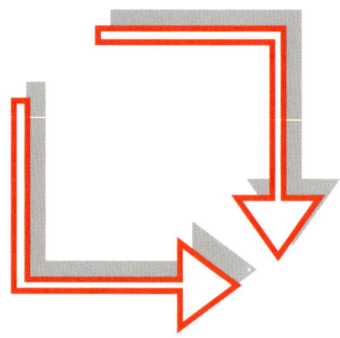

- **OPTICAL ILLUSIONS –** students look at and discuss a variety of optical illusions.

- **MAPPING –** students plot out multiple routes between two points on an actual map.

STOP-ABILITY ACTIVITIES-
for classroom transitions, homework, Math, and Social Skills.

STOP-ABILITY activities *assist the student in the quick shifting of topics. Students will have to quickly "shift" their cognitive thinking in response to changes in the game.*

- **TELEPHONE GAME -** students have to shift quickly between topics when a different "telephone" rings.

- **SPOT IT –** card game where you race to find the matching symbol between 2 cards.

www.KandMCenter.com

Copyright ©2012 The K&M Center, Inc.

Student Name: Jane Smith

Start Date: May 24, 2012

Flexible Thinking
Sample
Progress Chart

	Easy	Moderate	Challenging
	🟩	🟨	🟥

Session	1	2	3	4	5	6	7	8	9	10	11	12	13	14	15	16	17	18	19	20	21	22	23	24
Crossing the Midline																								
Infinity Signs	1	1		2	2	2				2			3	3			3			3			3	
Simon Says								2											2		2	2		
Hand Tasks																				2		5		
Changing the Rules																								
Color Shift	1					1								2			2	2	2		2	2		
Direction Shift		1	1	1			1		1	1				1		1				2				
Shape Shift																	2	4				3	2	
Sorting	1			1								2	2								3	3		
The Set Game																								
Organizing Your Thoughts																								
Describe and Draw It			1				1		1	1					2		2		2				3	
Tower of Hanoi		3			3			3		4				4				4				5		
Different Ways to the Same Answer																								
Optical Illusions																								
Mapping																								
Stop-Ability																								
Telephone Game																								
Spot It																								

www.KandMCenter.com

Copyright ©2012 The K&M Center, Inc.

STUDENT NAME: _____   START DATE: _____

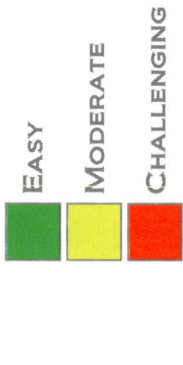

Flexible Thinking
Progress Chart

Easy | Moderate | Challenging

Session	1	2	3	4	5	6	7	8	9	10	11	12	13	14	15	16	17	18	19	20	21	22	23	24
Crossing the Midline																								
Infinity Signs																								
Simon Says																								
Hand Tasks																								
Changing the Rules																								
Color Shift																								
Direction Shift																								
Shape Shift																								
Sorting																								
The Set Game																								
Organizing Your Thoughts																								
Describe and Draw It																								
Tower of Hanoi																								
Different Ways to the Same Answer																								
Optical Illusions																								
Mapping																								
Stop-Ability																								
Telephone Game																								
Spot It																								

www.KandMCenter.com

Copyright ©2012 The K&M Center, Inc.

Flexible Thinking
Progress Chart

Student Name: _____ **Start Date:** _____

Easy 🟢 Moderate 🟡 Challenging 🔴

Session	25	26	27	28	29	30	31	32	33	34	35	36	37	38	39	40	41	42	43	44	45	46	47	48
Crossing the Midline																								
Infinity Signs																								
Simon Says																								
Hand Tasks																								
Changing the Rules																								
Color Shift																								
Direction Shift																								
Shape Shift																								
Sorting																								
The Set Game																								
Organizing Your Thoughts																								
Describe and Draw It																								
Tower of Hanoi																								
Different Ways to the Same Answer																								
Optical Illusions																								
Mapping																								
Stop-Ability																								
Telephone Game																								
Spot It																								

www.KandMCenter.com

Copyright ©2012 The K&M Center, Inc.

14

Strategy Recording Sheet

Use this sheet to record strategies that help you successfully complete the Flexible Thinking activities. Then, try using some of the same strategies in your schoolwork.

www.KandMCenter.com

Copyright ©2012 The K&M Center, Inc.

CROSSING THE MIDLINE

Infinity Signs

OBJECTIVE:
Students practice crossing their midline by tracing, writing, then air-drawing a variety of infinity signs.

TOOLS:
- Infinity Sheets 1-6
- Pencil, pen, or marker
- A blank sheet of paper

RULES:
⇨ *Do 1-3 rules each time you do this activity*

1. Student should first trace small infinity signs on Infinity Sheet 1 to get the "flow" of the infinity sign.
2. Students draw their own small infinity signs without a model to trace.
3. Students trace the large infinity sign on Infinity Sheet 2.
4. Students draw their own large infinity sign without a model to trace.
5. Students trace a variety of different-sized infinity signs on Infinity Sheet 3.
6. Students draw a variety of different-sized infinity signs on a blank sheet of paper.
7. Students practice tracing a variety of different sized infinity signs using Sheets 4-6.
8. Students "air-draw" large infinity signs with their dominant arm, then with their non-dominant arm.
9. Student can clasp hands together and "air-draw" the infinity sign with both arms.
10. Students "air-draw" the infinity sign with their left and/or right foot.
11. Students walk/jog the shape of the infinity sign in a large space such as an open room or yard.

INSTRUCTOR TIPS:
- Try using the "dotted" infinity signs if your student has trouble transitioning from tracing (e.g. Rule 1) to writing their own independently (e.g. Rule 2).
- Speak along with the student "middle, up, down, middle, up, down…."
- Some students benefit from having guidelines the first time they "air-draw." You can hold up two fists and have your student go around them (without touching) - like a race-track.

www.KandMCenter.com

Copyright ©2012 The K&M Center, Inc.

Crossing the Midline

INFINITY SIGNS

SHEET 1

www.KandMCenter.com

Copyright ©2012 The K&M Center, Inc.

Crossing the Midline

Sheet 1- Dotted

www.KandMCenter.com

Copyright ©2012 The K&M Center, Inc.

INFINITY SIGNS

Sheet 2

Crossing the Midline

www.KandMCenter.com

Copyright ©2012 The K&M Center, Inc.

Crossing the Midline

Infinity Signs

Sheet 2- Dotted

www.KandMCenter.com

Copyright ©2012 The K&M Center, Inc.

INFINITY SIGNS

SHEET 3

Crossing the Midline

www.KandMCenter.com

Copyright ©2012 The K&M Center, Inc.

Crossing the Midline

Sheet 4

www.KandMCenter.com

Copyright ©2012 The K&M Center, Inc.

CROSSING THE MIDLINE

INFINITY SIGNS

SHEET 5

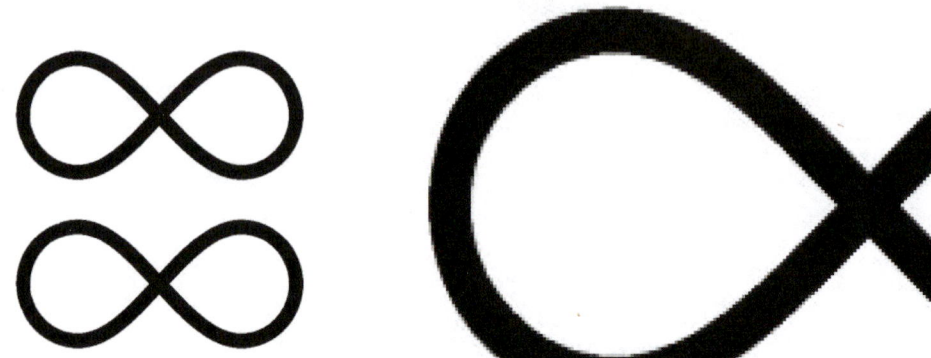

www.KandMCenter.com

Copyright ©2012 The K&M Center, Inc.

Crossing the Midline

Infinity Signs
Sheet 6

www.KandMCenter.com
Copyright ©2012 The K&M Center, Inc.

CROSSING THE MIDLINE

Simon Says

OBJECTIVE:
Students practice crossing their midline through the game of Simon Says.

TOOLS:
- "Crossing the Midline" Moves Sheet

HOW TO PLAY:
1. Instructor stands facing the student.
2. Tell the student that he/she should only follow the directions you give if you first say the words, "Simon Says."
3. Begin by saying something simple like, "Simon says, put your hands on your head."
4. Play standard "Simon Says" for a couple of rounds until you're certain the student knows the rules (without any midline crossing). Make sure to try some without saying "Simon says" to check on your student's understanding of the rules. For example:
   - Simon says, wave your hand.
   - Simon says, give a thumbs up.
   - Simon says, jump up and down.
   - Scratch your nose.
   - Simon says, pretend you're a tornado.
   - Sit on the ground.
5. Now try mixing in the "Crossing the Midline" Moves from the sheet so that with every "Simon says," your student is crossing their midline in some way.
6. Continue playing "Simon Says" with only "Crossing the Midline" Moves.

INSTRUCTOR TIPS:
- Practice the moves on the "Crossing the Midline" Moves Sheet prior to beginning so that you and your student know them without the pressure of the game.
- You can chose to gradually work up to all of the moves, by doing 5 a session OR you can teach all of the moves at the beginning.
- If remembering the moves is difficult, try making flash cards with illustrations that help the student remember what to do. For these students, make sure you're only introducing a couple of moves per game/session.
- To make it trickier, give the orders in rapid succession.
- Try cutting the orders short, saying "Simon Says, do this…." and then making the motion you want mimicked, such as putting your right hand on your left knee for Cross March.
- Alternate being Simon with your student. "Mess up" on purpose and see if your student can identify when the midline is NOT being crossed (e.g. incorrectly put your right hand on your right knee for Cross March).

www.KandMCenter.com

Copyright ©2012 The K&M Center, Inc.

CROSSING THE MIDLINE

"Crossing the Midline" Moves Sheet

Draw a line vertically down the middle of your body. That's called the midline. Every time you cross over that line, you are helping connect the hemispheres in your brain.

Practice all of these activities so that the student is familiar with all of the names and the movements associated with them. Once they are familiar, you can now begin using these motions in the game of Simon Says.

- TAP YOUR KNEE - Touch right hand to left knee and left hand to right knee.

- KNEE TO ELBOW - Lift left knee and touch with right elbow. Lift right knee and touch with left elbow.

- HAND TO FOOT - Lift left foot behind you and stretch back with right hand and touch. Reverse for the right foot and left hand.

- CROSS MARCH - Put the right hand on the left knee as you raise it, and then the left hand on the right knee, like marching.

- CATCH A STAR – Reach with right hand up in the air to your left and pretend to catch a star. Then reach with your left hand up in the air to your right and catch a star. (You can also pick apples, oranges, or any other fruit you like to eat.)

- WINDMILLS – Stretch out feet. Touch right hand to left foot. Stand. Touch left hand to right foot.

- PAT ON THE BACK – Alternate patting the back of your left shoulder with your right hand and your right shoulder with your left hand.

- PICKING CARROTS – Stand with feet stretched. Bend to the left and pretend to pull something beyond your left foot with your right hand. Stand. Bend to the right and pretend to pull something with your left hand.

- TUG OF WAR - Twist left and pretend to pull the rope towards you. Twist right and do the same.

- ROW THE BOAT – Put fists on top of each other as if holding an oar. Pretend to paddle on the right side of the body and then sweep hands and pretend to paddle on the left.

www.KandMCenter.com

Copyright ©2012 The K&M Center, Inc.

Crossing the Midline

- **Fill Your Shopping Cart** – Pretend to steer a grocery cart and then reach to the left with your right hand and take something off the shelf and put it in your cart. Reach with the left hand to the right and put something in the cart.

- **Climb the Ladder** – Act like you are climbing a ladder as you reach up with your right hand and lift your left knee. Reach with your left hand and lift your right knee.

- **Nose and Ears** – Touch right ear with left hand and place right hand on your nose. Touch left ear with right hand and place left hand on your nose.

- **Disco Dance** – Put right index finger in the air and point to the left. Bring right index finger down by your side. Place left index finger in the air and point to the right. Then bring down by your side.

- **Shoveling Snow** – Pretend to get a shovel and scoop up snow on the ground by your right foot. Throw the snow over your left shoulder. After ten times in this direction shovel snow from the left and throw it over your right shoulder.

- **Crazy Eights** – Make the figure eight in front of you with your right hand and then your left hand. Clasp your right and left hand and make large crazy eights.

- **Lazy Eights (infinity sign)** - Make "lazy" eights with your right hand. Make lazy eights with your left hand. Clasp your right and left hand and make large lazy eights.

www.KandMCenter.com

CROSSING THE MIDLINE

OBJECTIVE:
Students do a variety of movements with their left and right hands

TOOLS:
- Metronome (optional)

RULES:
⇨ Try 1-2 rules per session, going through motion 5-10 times:

1. The student should touch his or her thumb to each finger on ONE hand, starting with the pointer finger.
2. The student should touch his or her thumb to each finger on BOTH hands, starting with the pointer finger.
3. The student should touch their thumb to each finger from left to right with both hands at the same time (right thumb will touch pinkie first and left thumb will touch pointer first).
4. The student does Rule 2 WHILE saying the alphabet.
5. The student does Rule 2 with their arms crossed in front of them.
6. The student does Rule 3 WHILE saying the alphabet.
7. The student does Rule 3 WHILE having a conversation.
8. The student does Rule 3 with their arms crossed in front of them.
9. The student does Rule 3, BUT the student's right thumb should touch a finger on every beat and his or her left thumb should touch on every other beat (every time one thumb touches one finger, the other thumb touches two fingers).

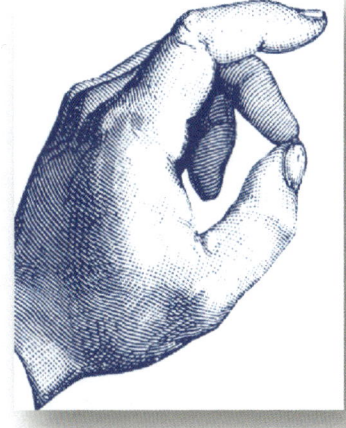

INSTRUCTOR TIPS:
- If your student has trouble, scaffold the activity by having them try one hand at a time.
- For a challenge, use a metronome to help your student keep a pace (try 120 beats per minute).

www.KandMCenter.com

Copyright ©2012 The K&M Center, Inc.

COLOR SHIFT

OBJECTIVE:
Student "reads" left to right through the color words based on the rule.
Student should be able to read 4-6 lines with accuracy.

TOOLS:
- Color Shift Activity Sheet

RULES:
⇨ Try 1-2 rules per session:

1. Student reads the **words**.
2. Student says the **color** the word is written in.
3. Student says the **color** the word is written in, but switching red for black, and black for red.
4. Student says the pattern (**color, word, color, word, color, word**, etc.).
5. Student says the pattern (**color, word, color, word, color, word**, etc.) but switching the colors red and green when saying the colors.

> Black... Blue... Red... Green...

> Red... Blue... Black... Green...

INSTRUCTOR TIPS:
- Student can say the rule aloud to themselves to help internalize it.
- Practice one line slowly to help fully understand the rule.
- For rules 2 and 3, blurring the words by squinting or slightly closing their eyes can help students NOT to read the words. This allows them to see "the big picture" rather than the details.
- A metronome can be used to help set a steady pace.
- Try the free **Stroop Effect** App available in The App Store.

www.KandMCenter.com

Copyright ©2012 The K&M Center, Inc.

Color Shift

Activity Sheet

Check to make sure all the words can be read:

Black	Blue	Green	Red
Black	Blue	Red	Black	Green	Red
Black	Black	Green	Black	Black	Green
Red	Black	Blue	Blue	Blue	Black
Black	Red	Green	Black	Black	Red
Green	Blue	Green	Blue	Blue	Green
Blue	Green	Red	Red	Green	Blue
Red	Great	Red	Green	Green	Red
Blue	Black	Blue	Green	Blue	Black
Blue	Black	Green	Green	Black	Green

Changing the Rules

www.KandMCenter.com

Copyright ©2012 The K&M Center, Inc.

CHANGING THE RULES

Direction Shift

OBJECTIVE:
Student "reads" left to right through the arrows based on the rule.
Student should be able to read 4-6 lines with accuracy.

TOOLS:
- Direction Shift Activity Sheet – COLOR
- Direction Shift Activity Sheet – Black & White

RULES:
⇨ Try 1-2 rules per session:

1. Student says the **colors** of the arrows.
2. Student says the **direction** of the arrows.
3. Student says the **colors** of the arrows but switching red for green and green for red.
4. Student says the **colors** of the "left" and "right" arrows but says the **direction** of the "up" and "down" arrows.
5. Student says the pattern (**color, color, direction, color, color, direction**, etc.) of the arrows.
6. Student says the pattern (**color, direction, color, direction**, etc.) of the arrows.

> Black... Blue... Blue... Red....

> Left... Down... Right... Up...

> Black... Blue... Blue... Green....

INSTRUCTOR TIPS:
- Student can say the rule aloud to themselves to help internalize it.
- Practice one line slowly to help fully understand the rule.
- For rules 1 and 3, blurring by squinting or slightly closing their eyes can help students NOT see the direction of the arrows. This allows them to see "the big picture" rather than the details.
- A metronome can be used to help set a steady pace.

www.KandMCenter.com

Copyright ©2012 The K&M Center, Inc.

Direction Shift

Activity Sheet – Color

Make sure students can determine the direction of the arrows:

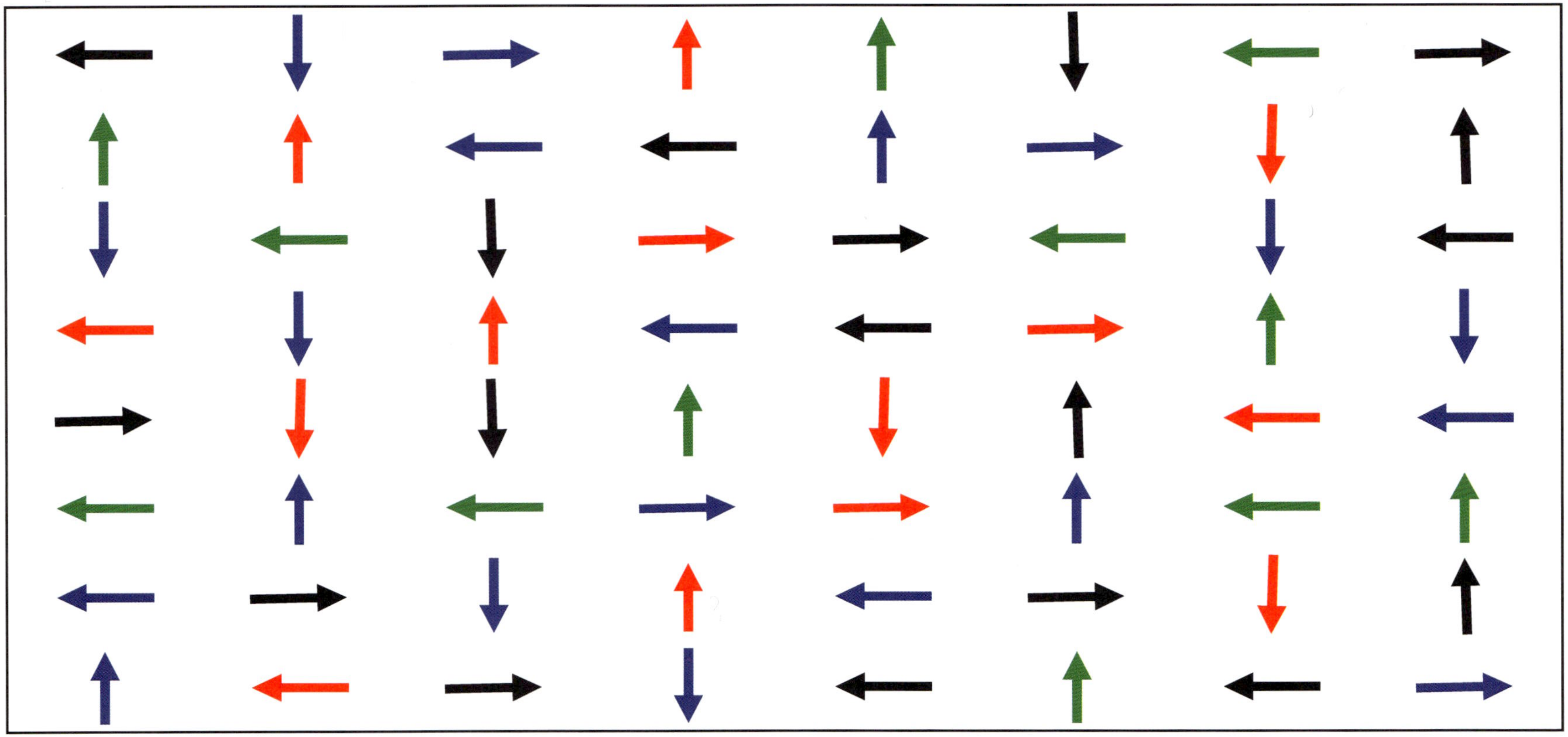

→ Down
← Up
↑ Right
↓ Left

www.KandMCenter.com

Copyright ©2012 The K&M Center, Inc.

Changing the Rules

Direction Shift

Activity Sheet – Black & White

Make sure students can determine the direction of the arrows:

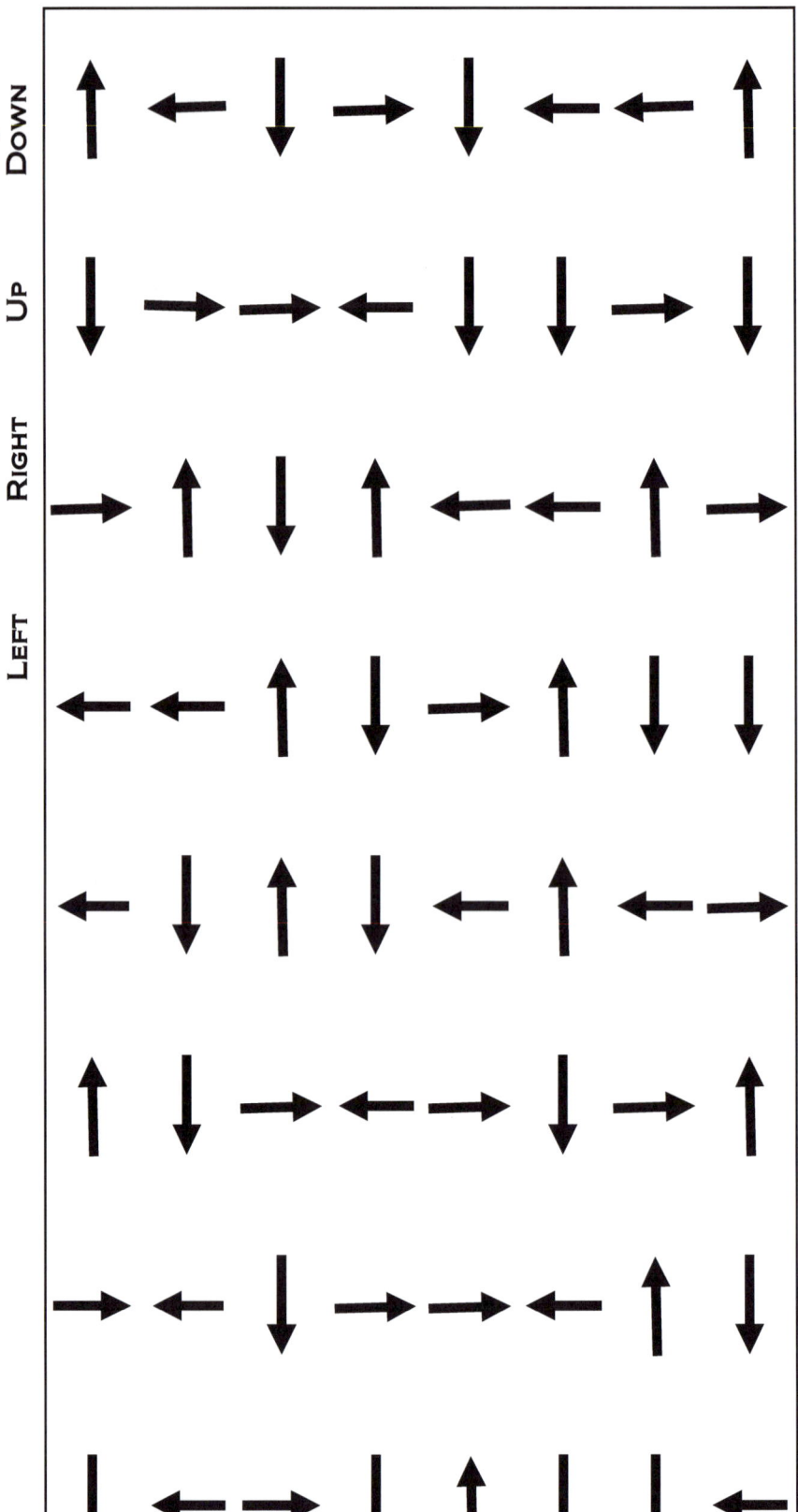

↓ Left   ↑ Right   ↑ Up   → Down

↑	←	↓	→	↓	←	←	↑
↓	→	→	←	↓	↓	→	↓
→	↑	↓	↑	←	←	↑	→
←	←	↑	↓	→	↑	↓	↓
←	↓	↑	↓	←	↑	←	↔
↑	↓	→	←	→	↓	→	↑
→	←	↓	→	←	←	↑	↓
↓	←	→	↓	↑	↓	↓	←

www.KandMCenter.com

Copyright ©2012 The K&M Center, Inc.

Changing the Rules

Shape Shift

Directions

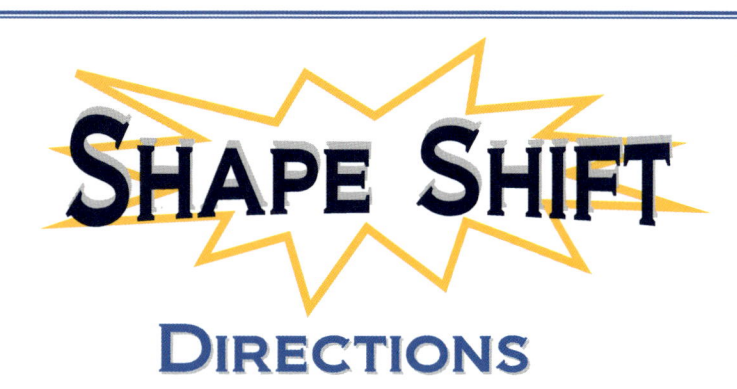

Objective:
Student "reads" left to right through the shapes based on the rule. Student should be able to read 4-6 lines with accuracy.

Tools:
- Shape Shift Activity Sheet

Rules:
⇨ Try 1-2 rules per session:

1. Student says the **shape**.
2. Student says if the shape is **shaded** or **unshaded**.
3. Student says the **shape** of the ovals and **shaded/unshaded** for the triangles.
4. Student says the **shape** of the triangle and **shaded/unshaded** for the ovals.
5. Student says the pattern (**shape, shading, shape, shading**, etc.)
6. Student says the **shape**, but switching ovals for triangles and triangles for ovals.

> Triangle... Oval...
> Oval... Triangle...

> Unshaded... Unshaded...
> Unshaded... Unshaded...

> Unshaded... Oval...
> Oval... Unshaded...

Instructor Tips:
- Student can say the rule aloud to themselves.
- Practice one line slowly to help fully understand the rule.
- A metronome can be used to help set a steady pace.

www.KandMCenter.com

Copyright ©2012 The K&M Center, Inc.

Shape Shift

Activity Sheet

Make sure students know these shapes:

Triangle △   Oval ◯

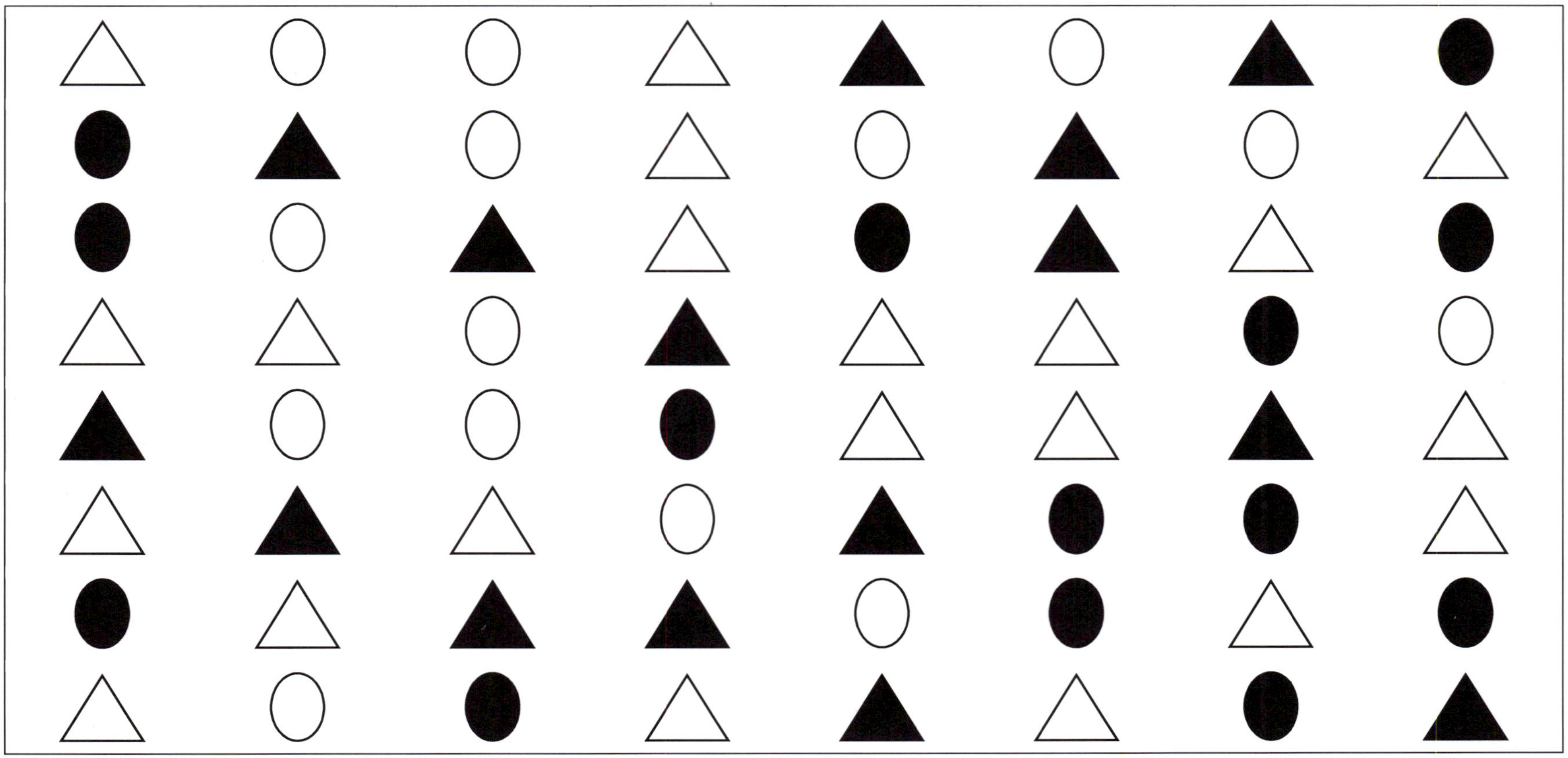

CHANGING THE RULES

SORTING

OBJECTIVE:
Students sort each deck of cards based on a variety of characteristics.

TOOLS:
- Sorting Cards Deck 1
- Sorting Cards Deck 2
- Sorting Cards Deck 3

RULES:
⇨ Do one deck at a time

1. After cutting out the cards for each deck, ask your student to sort the cards from Deck 1 into 2 groups as many ways as they can.
2. You can tell them that there are at least 5 ways to sort the cards, but try not to tell them the ways (shape of card, font of word in card, clothing/transportation, shading, etc.).
3. Have your student verbalize how they sorted. For example, "these are all in capital letters" or "this pile has animals and that pile has things you wear."
4. Follow the same procedure for Deck 2 and Deck 3.

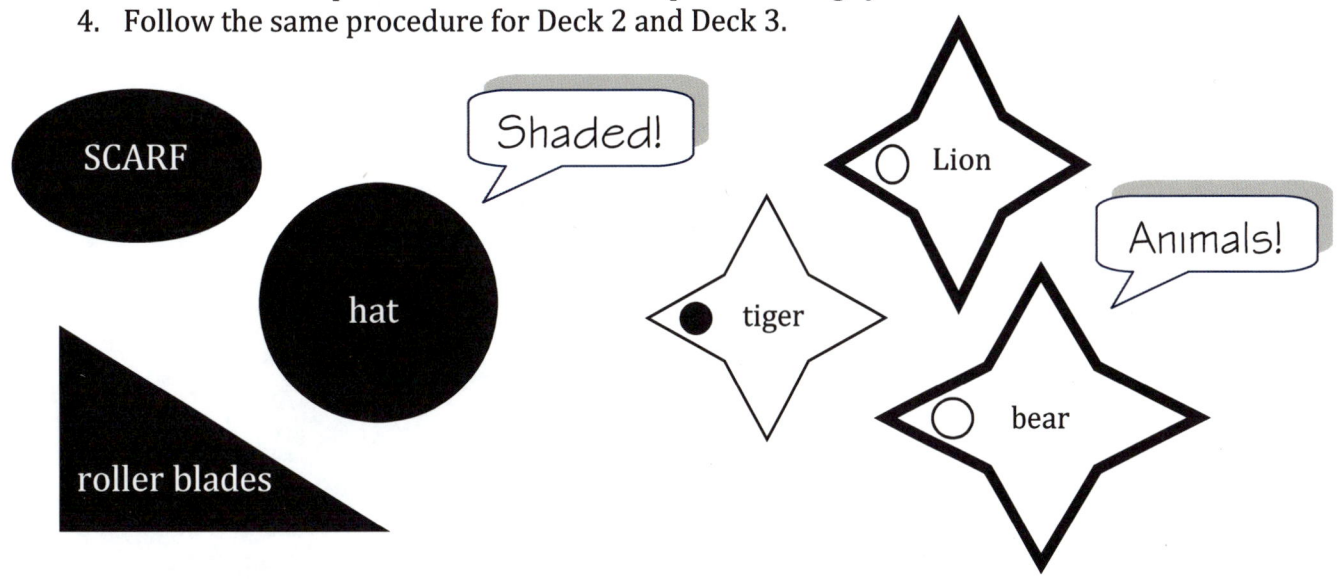

INSTRUCTOR TIPS:
- If your student gets stuck, find 2 that go together and ask what the 3rd would be. Then ask your student to tell you how he/she sorted them.
- Make your own sorting activity by sorting any number of different items around the house in different ways.

www.KandMCenter.com

Copyright ©2012 The K&M Center, Inc.

Sorting

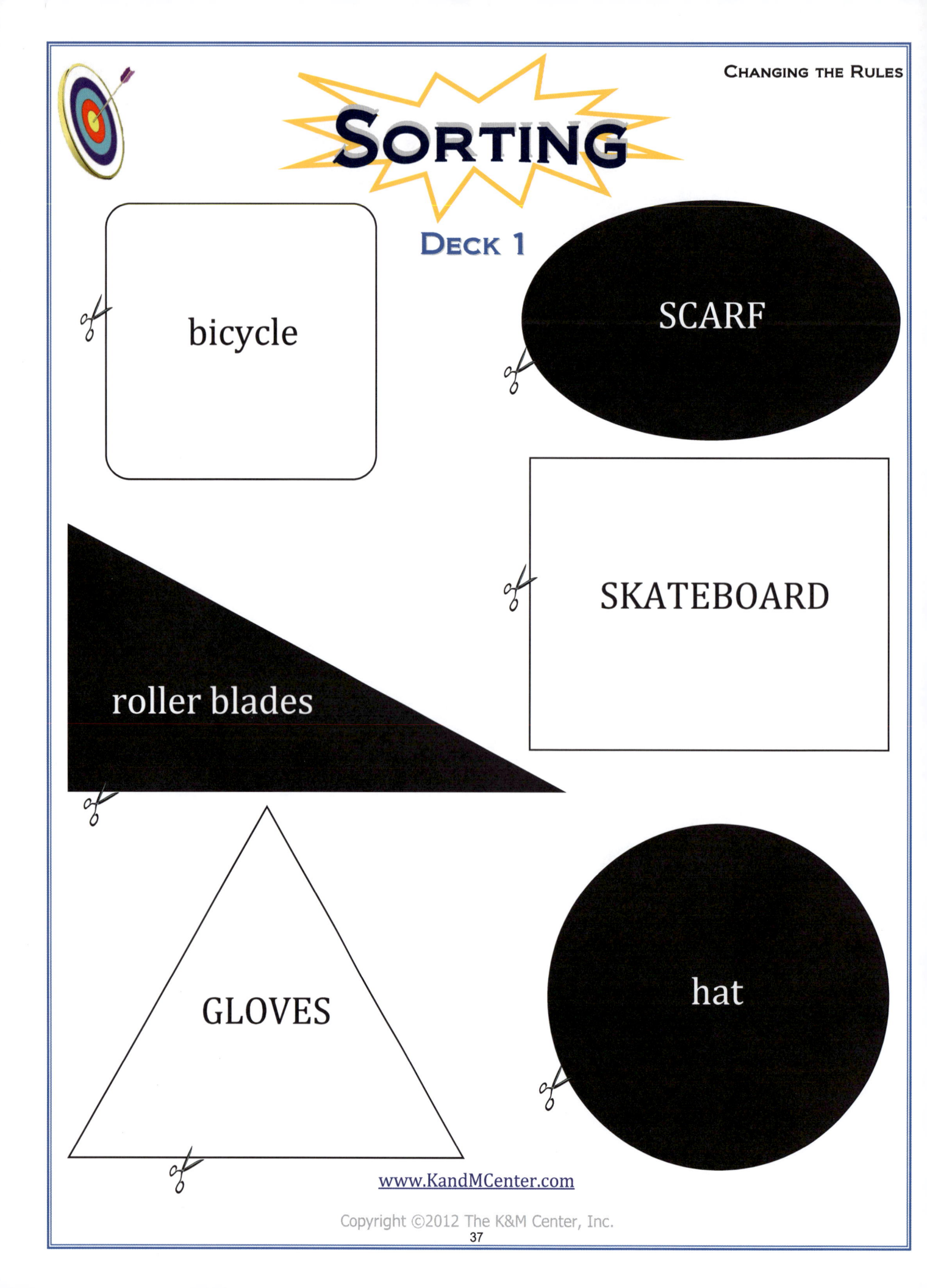

Deck 1

bicycle

SCARF

SKATEBOARD

roller blades

GLOVES

hat

www.KandMCenter.com

Changing the Rules

Copyright ©2012 The K&M Center, Inc.

SORTING

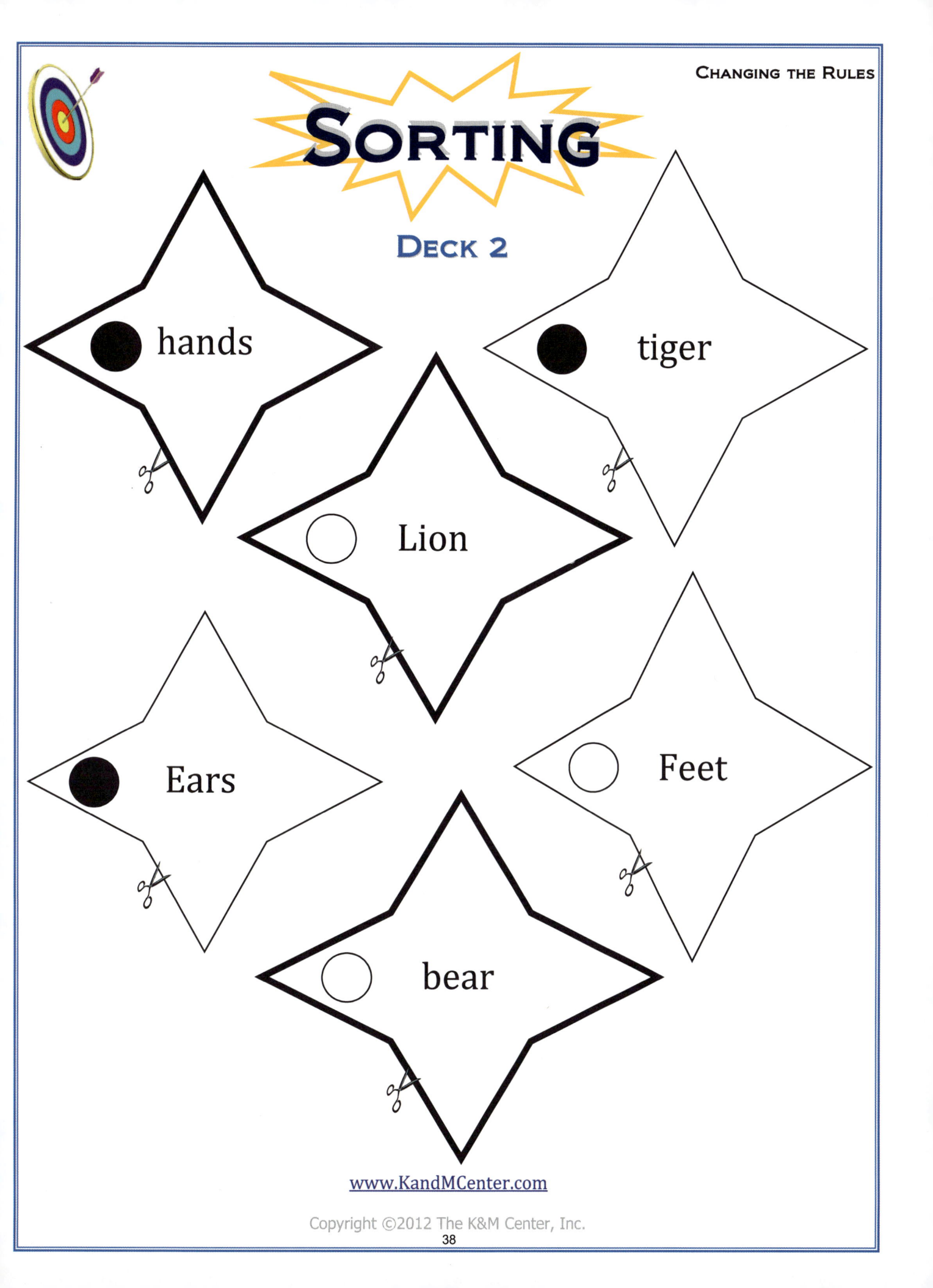

Deck 2

- hands
- tiger
- Lion
- Ears
- Feet
- bear

Changing the Rules

www.KandMCenter.com

Copyright ©2012 The K&M Center, Inc.

SORTING

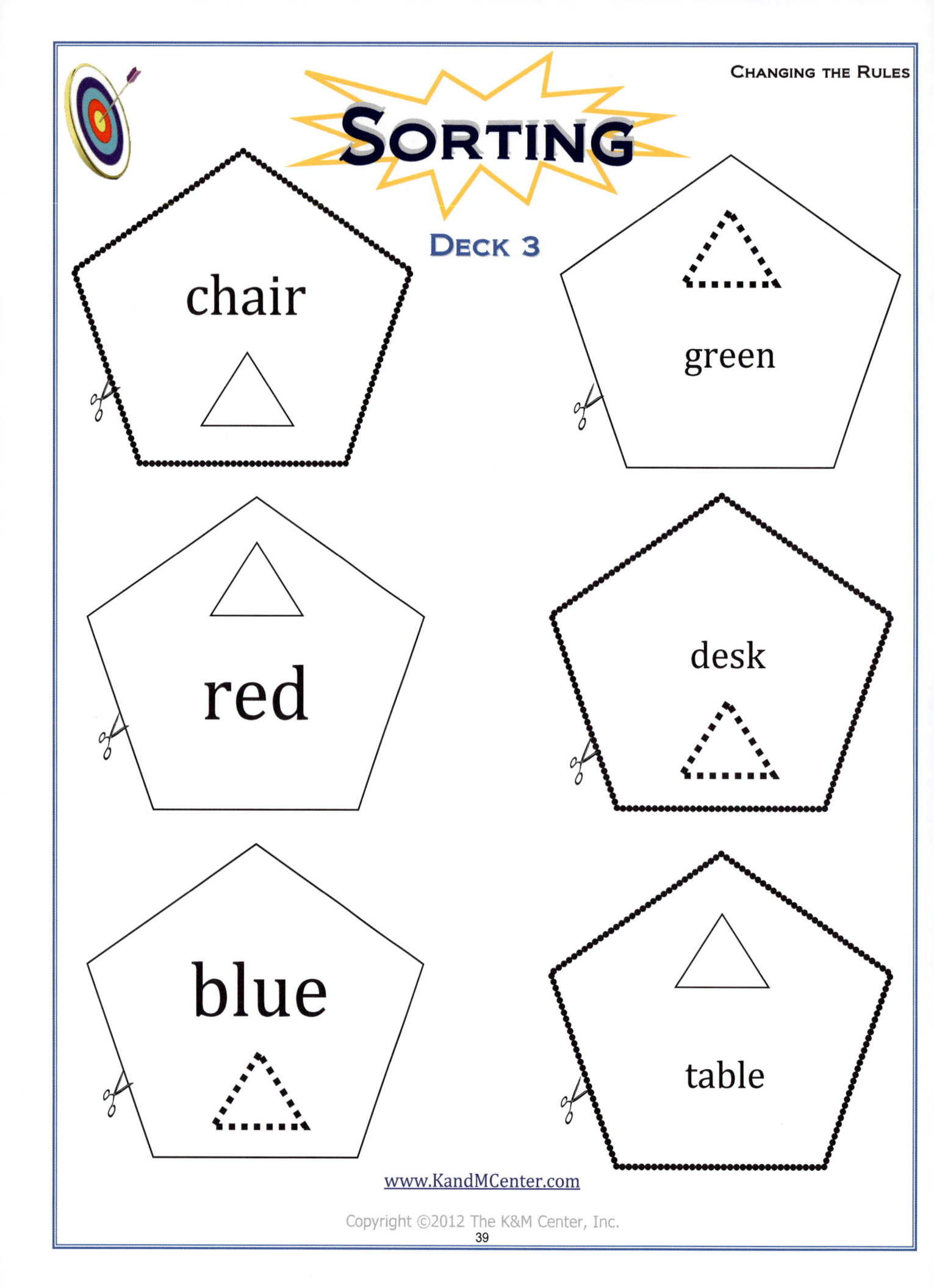

Deck 3

Changing the Rules

- chair
- green
- red
- desk
- blue
- table

www.KandMCenter.com

Copyright ©2012 The K&M Center, Inc.

CHANGING THE RULES

THE SET GAME

OBJECTIVE:
Make "sets" of three cards whose characteristics (shape, color, number, shading) is ALL the same or ALL different.

TOOLS:
- The Set Game (www.kandmcenter.com/the_store/index.cfm?fuseaction=product.display&product_ID=8) or a computer with the internet

INSTRUCTIONS:
1. Watch an instructional video online: http://www.setgame.com/set/index.html or read the instructions included with the game.
2. Play The Set Game with 12 cards out at a time.
3. Once a "set" is made, the 3 cards may be collected by whoever made the set. 3 cards are put down to replace the ones that were taken.
4. A Daily Set Game can also be played online here:
   http://www.setgame.com/set/puzzle_frame.htm
   or http://www.nytimes.com/ref/crosswords/setpuzzle.html

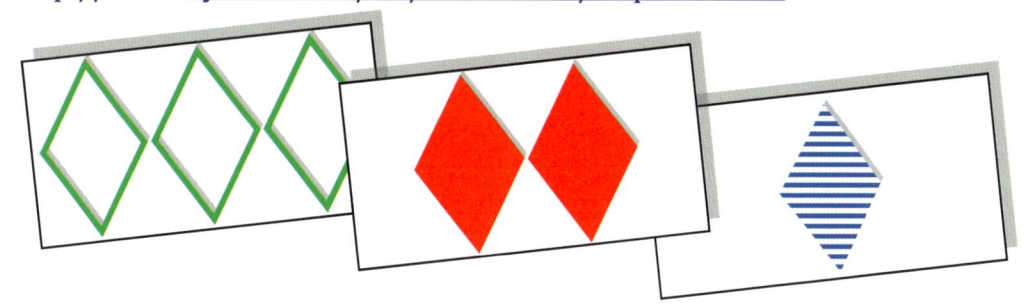

INSTRUCTOR TIPS:
- When first learning The Set Game, show students 2 cards and challenge them to find the 3rd card in the "set" (allowing them to look throughout the whole deck to find it).
- Try only putting down cards that are solidly colored. That way you are removing one of the characteristics students have to match.
- Encourage students to look for cards that are "all the same" in one way (all red or all triangles) to help narrow down their search.
- Have student choose 2 cards out of the 12 and then have them see if the 3rd one in the "set" is there.
- Separate the 12 cards into 3 groups: cards with 1 shape, cards with 2 shapes, and cards with 3 shapes. It's easier to spot "sets" this way.

www.KandMCenter.com

Copyright ©2012 The K&M Center, Inc.

ORGANIZING YOUR THOUGHTS

Describe and Draw

Objective:
Given a shape, student will be able to verbally describe it to instructor. Instructor draws what student says and it should accurately reflect the picture the student was describing.

Tools:
- Describe and Draw Activity Sheets
- Paper
- Pencil
- Colored Markers (optional)

Instructions:
⇨ begin with Level 1 Describe and Draw Sheet

1. Show the student all the shapes on a Level 1 Describe and Draw Sheet. Ask them to pick one shape, but not to tell you which one it is.
2. Explain to the student that they are going to describe to you the shape they've chosen, using only their words (no hand movements or "showing"). While they describe it, you are going to draw what they say.
3. As the student describes, be sure to draw what they say, in a very literal sense. If they say "draw a square" make sure you draw a square, however if they don't specify size, then draw a really large or really small square. If your student says "draw a triangle" try making a really tall, thin triangle. They may assume that you know the general size and direction because you saw the sheet as well, so the very first time you do the activity, you've got to tell them that you are going on purely what they say, not on what you might have seen on the sheet.
4. When they're done describing, compare the picture you drew to the one being described. Ask your student: What did you do a good job of describing? What could you have been more specific about?
5. Once your student is able to accurately describe shapes from the Level 1 sheet, move on to Level 2 and then Level 3.
6. Students can make their own Describe and Draw sheets with clip art or doodles.

www.KandMCenter.com

Organizing your Thoughts

INSTRUCTOR TIPS:

- Remind students to take their time and to think about the order of directions before he/she states them.
- Use the "Stop, Think, Plan, Do" visual to help students remember to take their time to formulate a plan.
- If students struggle with finding words, make a word bank together of words that could describe all of the shapes on the page (circle, rectangle, star, perpendicular, on the right side, on top, inside, outside).
- Encourage students to describe the "big picture" first. That may mean the largest shape (draw the outline of a square with sides each approximately 4" long) or the basic outline (draw the profile of a high-top sneaker facing to the right).
- Model describing by switching roles with the student acting as artist while you give the descriptions.
- You can use pictures/clipart to create your own Describe and Draw sheets to continue practice.
- After completion, discuss with student how they could have made their directions clearer. Write down those suggestions and use them next time you do the activity.

www.KandMCenter.com

ORGANIZING YOUR THOUGHTS

DESCRIBE AND DRAW

LEVEL 1 SHAPES

www.KandMCenter.com

Copyright ©2012 The K&M Center, Inc.

ORGANIZING YOUR THOUGHTS

DESCRIBE AND DRAW

LEVEL 1 SHAPES

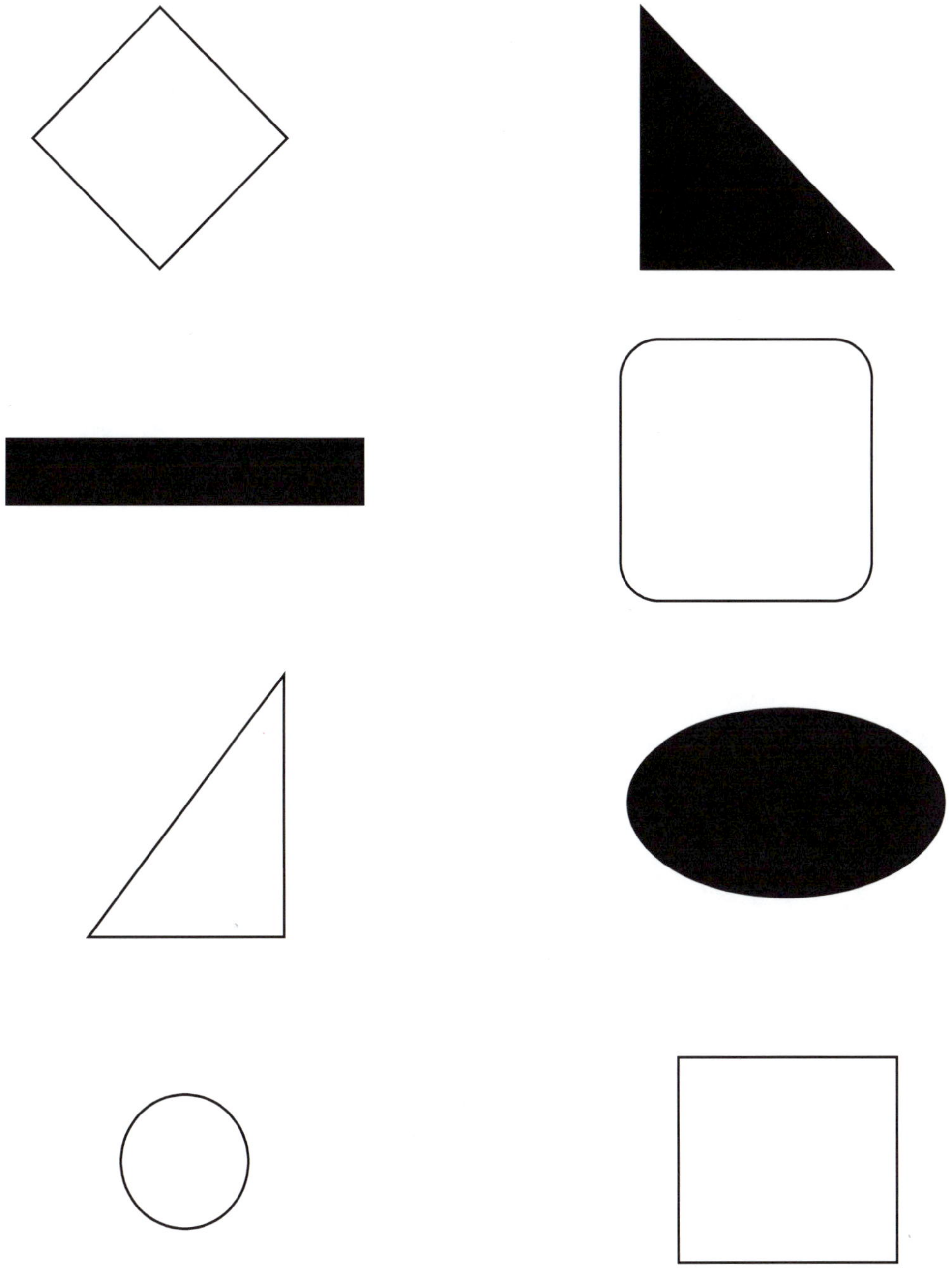

www.KandMCenter.com

ORGANIZING YOUR THOUGHTS

DESCRIBE AND DRAW

LEVEL 2 SHAPES

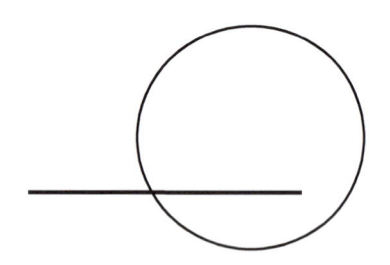

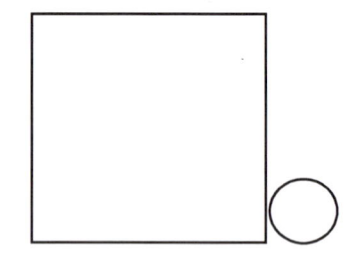

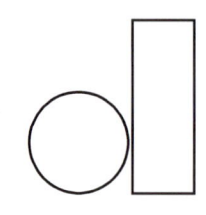

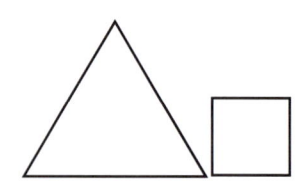

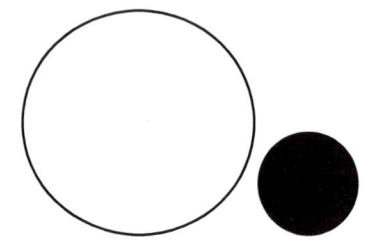

www.KandMCenter.com

Copyright ©2012 The K&M Center, Inc.

ORGANIZING YOUR THOUGHTS

DESCRIBE AND DRAW

LEVEL 2 SHAPES

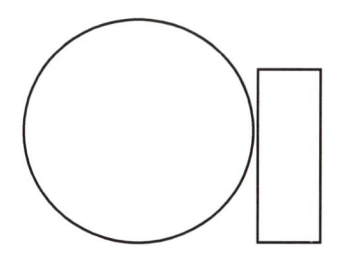

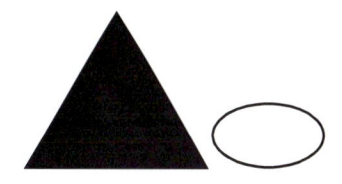

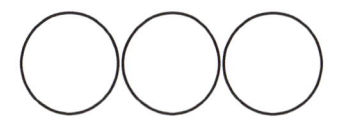

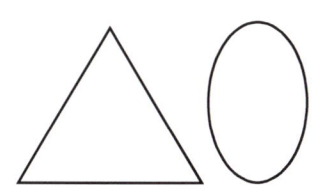

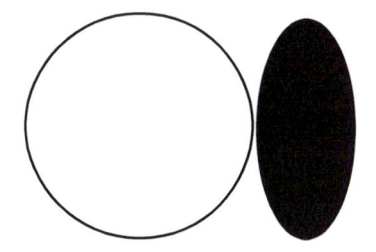

ORGANIZING YOUR THOUGHTS

DESCRIBE AND DRAW

LEVEL 3 SHAPES

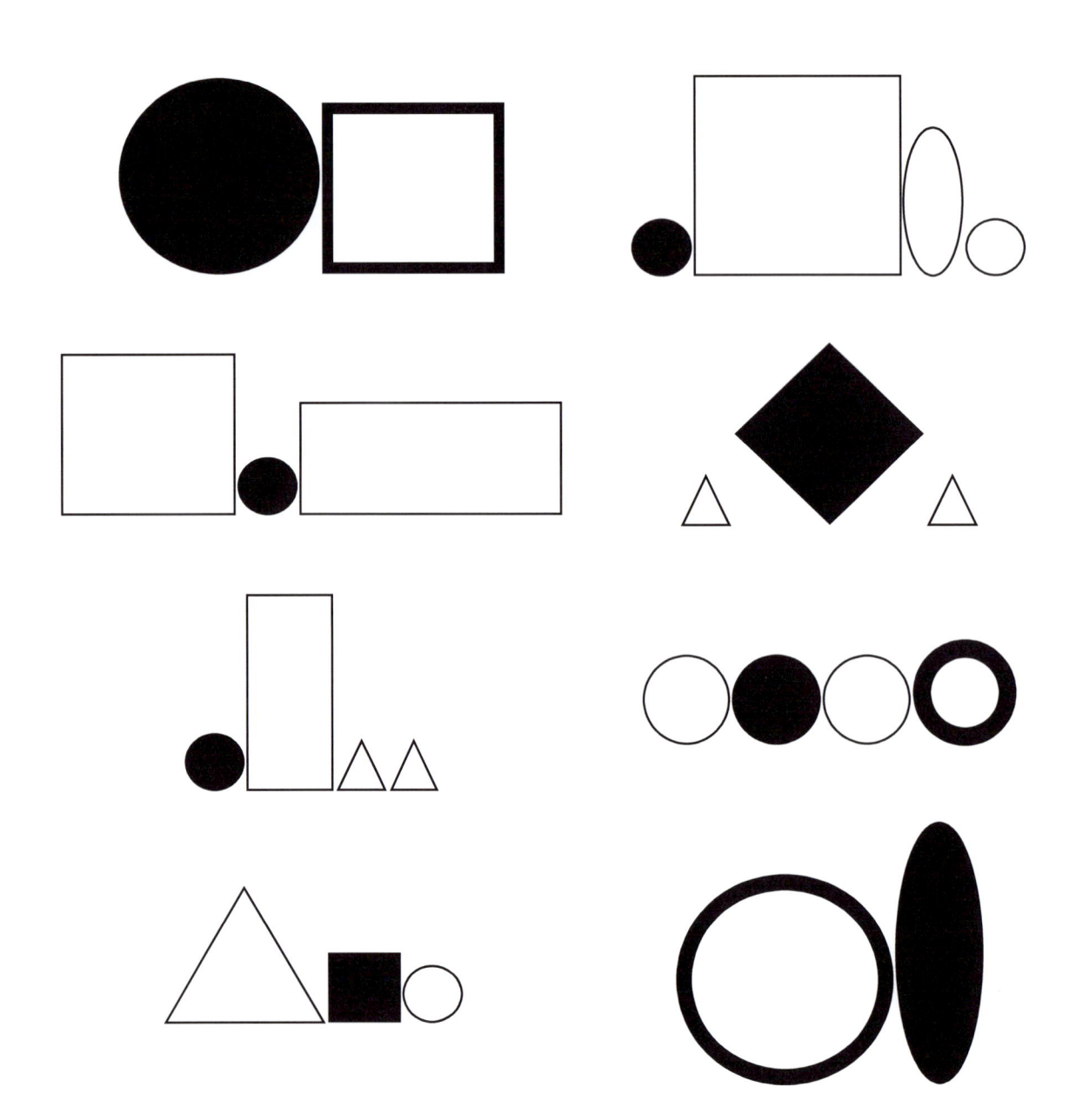

www.KandMCenter.com

Copyright ©2012 The K&M Center, Inc.

Describe and Draw

Level 3 Shapes

www.KandMCenter.com

ORGANIZING YOUR THOUGHTS

TOWER OF HANOI

OBJECTIVE:
Student moves the rings, one at a time,
from the rod furthest to the left to the rod furthest to the right,
recreating the original conical shape.

TOOLS:
- Computer with internet access*- http://www.mazeworks.com/hanoi/

INSTRUCTIONS:
⇨ begin with 3 discs

1. Only one disk may be moved at a time. Each move consists of taking the upper disk from one of the rods and sliding it onto another rod on top of the other disks that may already be present on that rod. No disk may be placed on top of a smaller disk.
2. Students should first concentrate on solving the puzzle and understanding the rules of the challenge.
3. Once they have done 3 disks successfully, encourage them to try to do it in the least amount of moves (can be found by watching the "Solution").
4. After they have mastered 3 disks, move on to 4 disks, following the same procedures.
5. After they have mastered 4 disks, have them keep practicing by challenging them to 5 disks, 6 disks, 7 disks, etc.

INSTRUCTOR TIPS:
- Try watching the "Solution" (at a slow speed) to study what the moves are.
- Remind students that sometimes you have to make a move that seems counter-productive to solve the puzzle.
- If stuck, encourage students to "Restart," a great strategy when they're feeling overwhelmed and confused.
- Try the free Tap Towers app available in The App Store.

*Adult supervision is suggested for any web-based activities.

www.KandMCenter.com

Copyright ©2012 The K&M Center, Inc.

Different Ways to the Same Answer

Optical Illusions

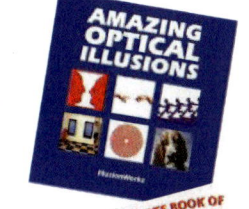

Objective:
Student should be able to recognize multiple images in one picture.

Tools:
- Optical Illusions pages
- Optical Illusions books: <u>The Ultimate Book of Optical Illusions by Al Seckel</u>
  <u>Amazing Optical Illusions by IllusionWorks</u> 
- Optical Illusion websites*: Illusions.org
  An Optical Illusion (www.anopticalillusion.com)
  NIEHS Kids' Pages (kids.niehs.nih.gov/games/illusions/index.htm)

Instructions:
1. Start by looking at the first image (saxophone/woman's face) with your student. Ask them what they see first.
2. Tell your student that this is what is called an "ambiguous illusion" because it is open to more than one interpretation or has a "double meaning." In other words, there is another picture hidden inside if you look at it in a different way.
3. Ask your student to "see" the other picture. If they get stuck, you can tell them what to look for. For example, "there is also a woman's face in this picture."
4. Discuss the images so you're sure your student is actually "seeing" both images.
5. Move on to the next pages following the same instructions.

Instructor Tips:
- If a student has difficulty "seeing" another image in the picture, cover up certain parts of the picture and trace the outline of the image with your finger.
- If a student is having difficulty, try holding up the picture from across the room and having them look at the picture from a distance. Sometimes a different perspective can help!
- Try having your student squint their eyes if they cannot "see" the alternate image.
- Try having your student switch their thinking about a picture WHILE they're looking at it. For example, have them "see" the saxophonist, then have them "see" the woman, then "see" the saxophonist again.
- Print out 2 copies of one image and have your student color them in 2 different ways. For example, color one image as if it were the "duck" and then color the same image as if it were the "rabbit."

* Adult supervision is suggested for any web-based activities.

www.KandMCenter.com

Copyright ©2012 The K&M Center, Inc.

Different Ways to the Same Answer

Optical Illusions

Image Source: Wikimedia Commons
Mooney Face Picture: An example of the face photographs used by the cognitive psychologist Craig Mooney.

- Do you see a saxophonist?

- Do you see a woman's face?

www.KandMCenter.com

Copyright ©2012 The K&M Center, Inc.

Different Ways to the Same Answer

Optical Illusions

IMAGE SOURCE: Wikimedia Commons
IMAGE BY: Brocken Inaglory

- Do you see two silhouette profiles?

- Do you see a white vase?

www.KandMCenter.com

Different Ways to the Same Answer

Optical Illusions

IMAGE SOURCE: Wikimedia Commons
My Wife and My Mother-In-Law: by the cartoonist W. E. Hill, 1915
(adapted from a picture going back at least to a 1888 German postcard).

- Do you see an old woman with her chin down?

- Do you see a young woman with her head turned?

www.KandMCenter.com

Copyright ©2012 The K&M Center, Inc.

Different Ways to the Same Answer

Optical Illusions

Image by: Peter Brookes, 1979

- Do you see a cat?

- Do you see a mouse?

www.KandMCenter.com

Copyright ©2012 The K&M Center, Inc.

Different Ways to the Same Answer

Optical Illusions

Image Source: Jastrow, J. (1899). The mind's eye.
Popular Science Monthly, **54**, 299-312. From Wikimedia Commons
Duck Rabbit Illusion

- Do you see a duck looking to the left?

- Do you see a rabbit looking to the right?

www.KandMCenter.com

Copyright ©2012 The K&M Center, Inc.

Different Ways to the Same Answer

Optical Illusions

IMAGE BY: Charles Allan Gilbert
All is Vanity, 1892

- Do you see a woman looking in the mirror?

- Do you see a skull?

www.KandMCenter.com

Copyright ©2012 The K&M Center, Inc.

DIFFERENT WAYS TO THE SAME ANSWER

MAPPING

OBJECTIVE:
Student finds multiple routes between two points on a map.

TOOLS:
- Map Print-outs,
- Green marker
- Yellow Marker
- Red Marker
- Computer with internet

INSTRUCTIONS:
⇨ begin with the maps provided

1. Show your student the two points on the map that they are to find a route between.
2. Explain to them that they are to find what they think is the shortest route between the 2 points. They have to stay on marked roads.
3. Encourage students to look and think about their route before they start writing on the map. It is not a "maze" and shouldn't be solved like one.
4. They can draw what they think the fastest route is using the green marker.
5. Next, they are to find another *different* route between the same 2 points. They can draw that route in yellow.
6. Have the students find a third route between the 2 points. They can draw that route in red.
7. Hold the completed map away from the student and have look and see if their green line does in fact look shorter than their yellow and red lines.
8. On google maps, put in the 2 points and check and see if the student's "green" route was in fact the shortest route.
9. Repeat these steps with the maps provided.
10. Find and print out your own maps or use the Skitch app with google maps to continue practicing this activity.

www.KandMCenter.com

MAPPING

Different Ways to the Same Answer

INSTRUCTOR TIPS:
- Try a variety of locations both familiar (their neighborhood) and unfamiliar (a different state) to the student.
- Encourage your student to think about (or even draw) different routes they could get from one room to another room within their school or home.
- Hold the completed map away from the student and have look and see if their green line does in fact look shorter than their yellow and red lines.
- If they like, students can find a fourth route that is long and winding (staying on the page). It can be the "Ridiculous Route" and done in a different color.

www.KandMCenter.com

MAPPING

Map #1

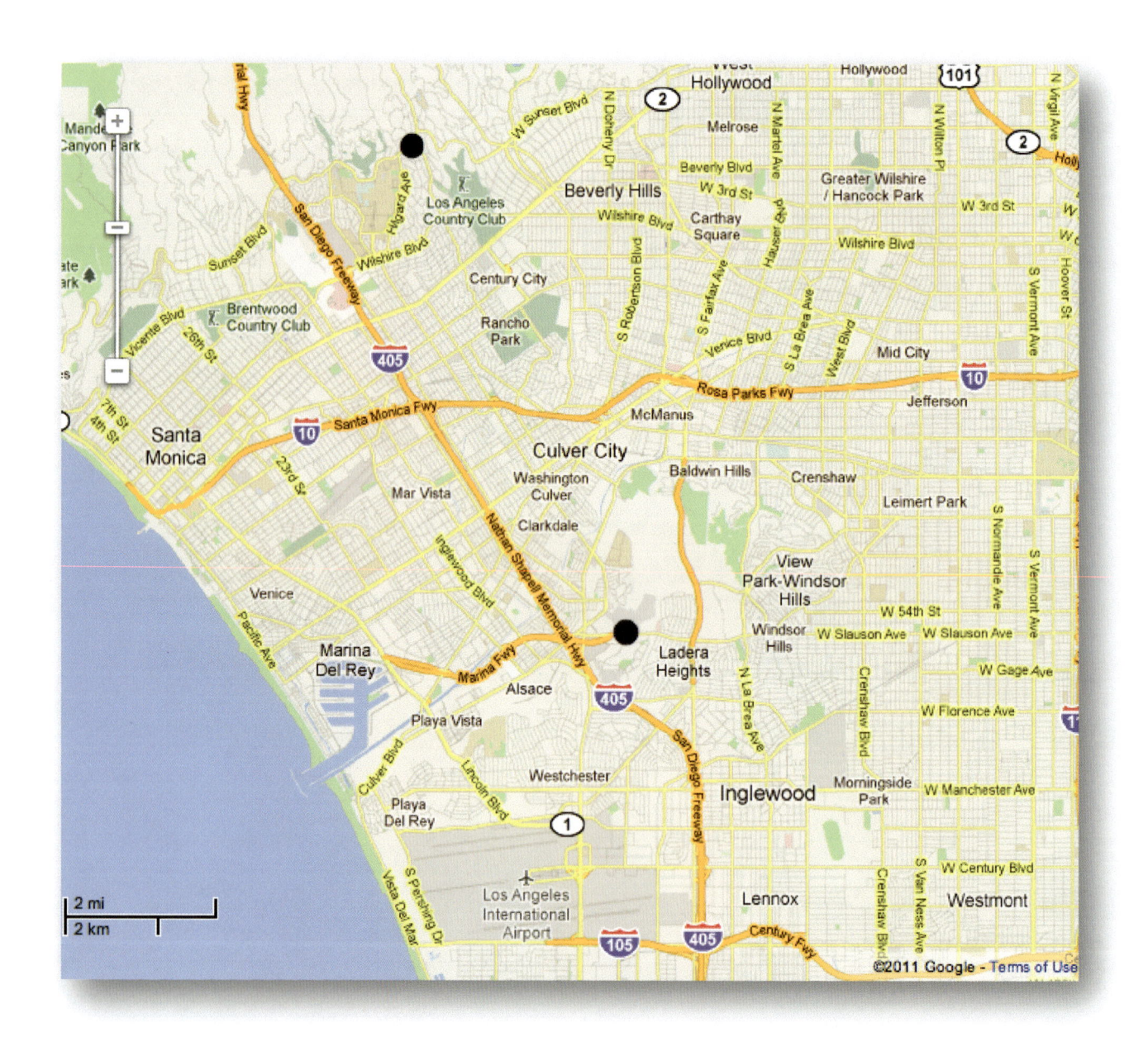

www.KandMCenter.com

DIFFERENT WAYS TO THE SAME ANSWER

MAPPING

MAP #2

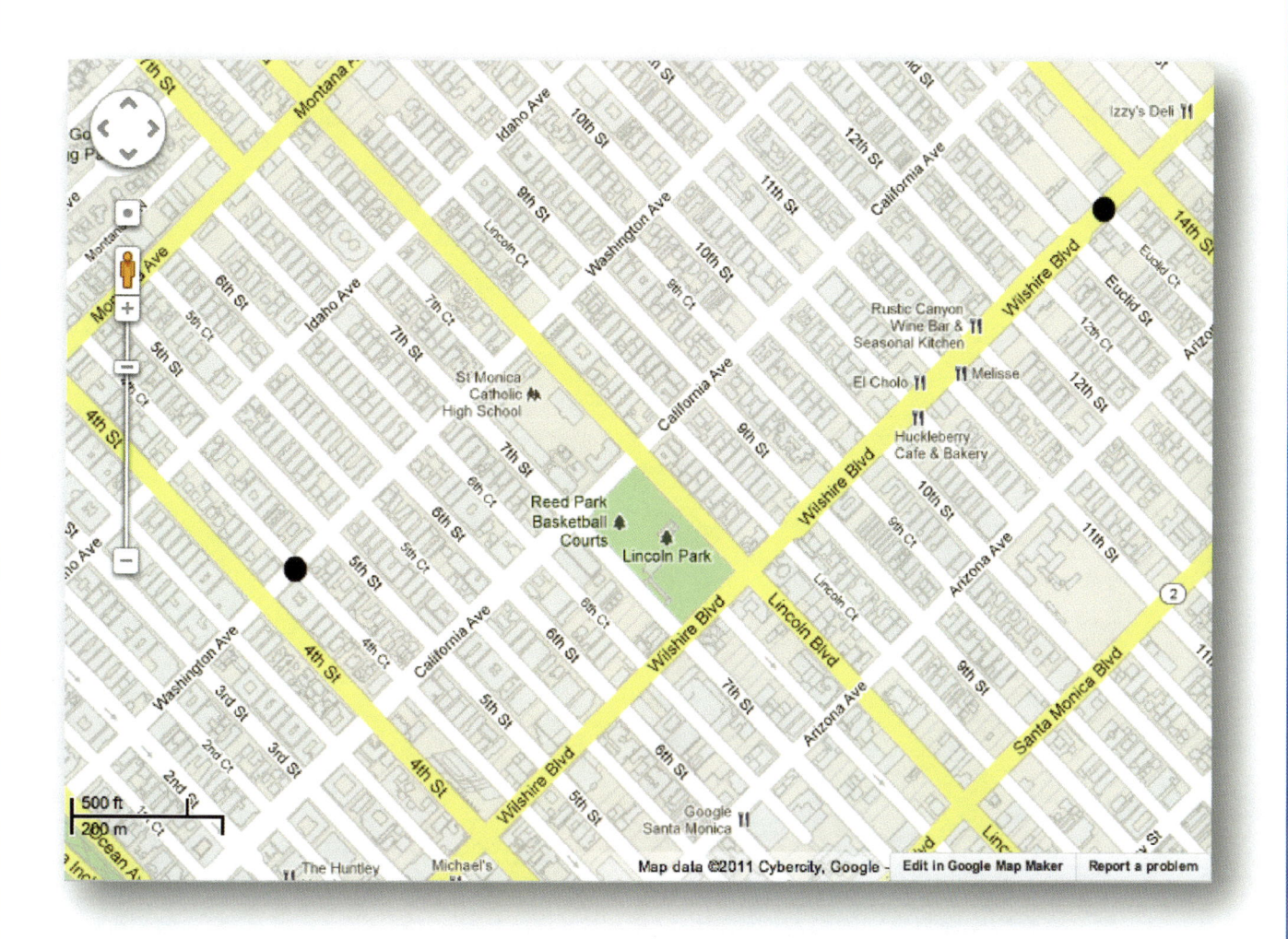

www.KandMCenter.com

Copyright ©2012 The K&M Center, Inc.

DIFFERENT WAYS TO THE SAME ANSWER

MAPPING

MAP #3

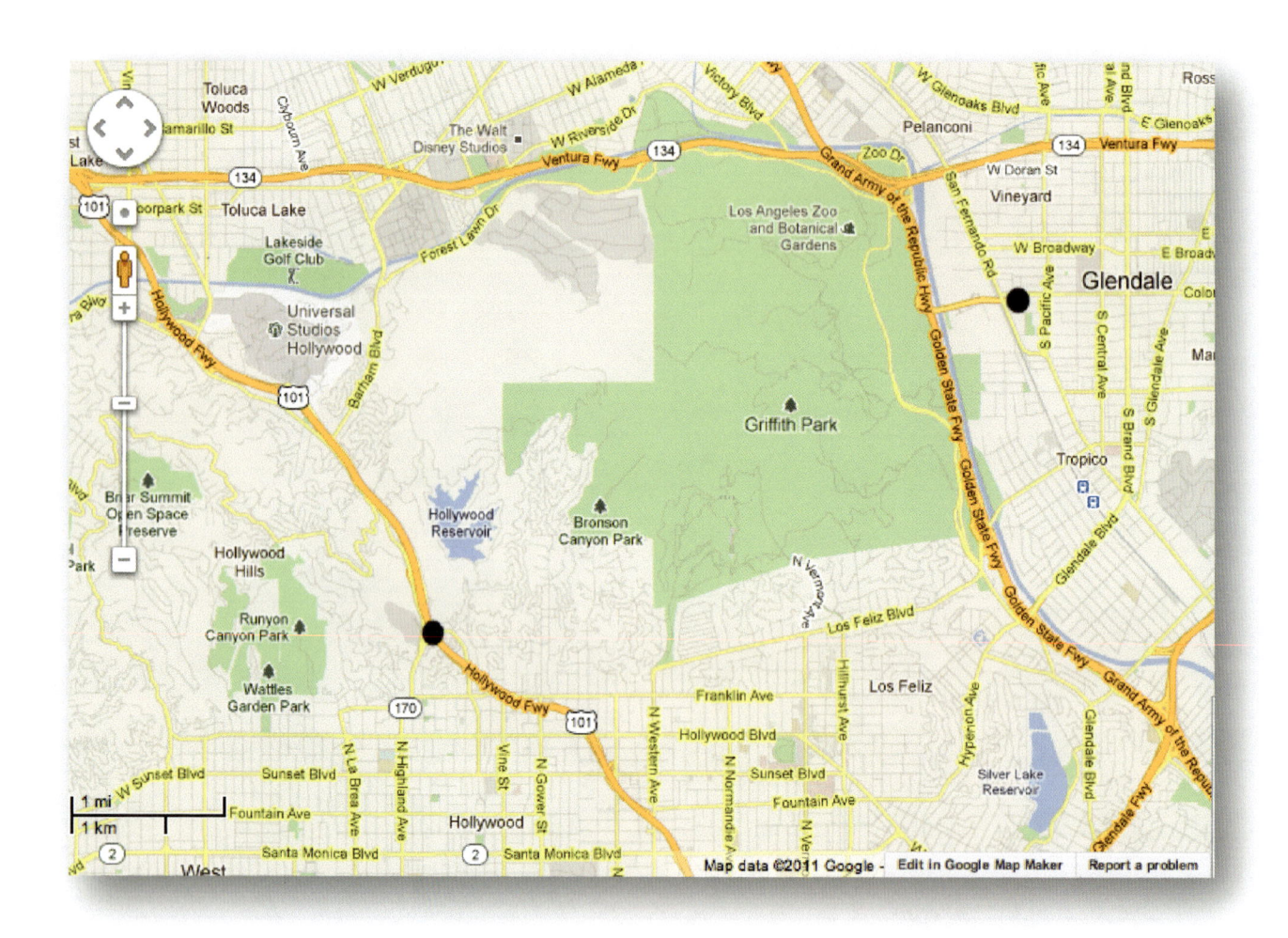

www.KandMCenter.com

Copyright ©2012 The K&M Center, Inc.

STOP-ABILITY

Brainstorm some activities that are *easy* to STOP:
_____
_____
_____

...and some activities that are *harder* to STOP:
_____
_____
_____

Whether I am at school, with friends, or at home, it's important to be able to STOP when time is up. It is important because:

1. _____
2. _____

For example, once I had to STOP _____ so that I could _____
_____.

Another time I had to STOP _____ so that I could _____
_____.

I can either choose to STOP myself or _____
_____.

When I don't get to STOP myself, I feel _____
_____.

To help me to STOP by myself, I can:

1. _____
2. _____
3. _____

www.KandMCenter.com

Copyright ©2012 The K&M Center, Inc.

STOP-ABILITY

TELEPHONE GAME

OBJECTIVE:
Students practice stopping talking about one topic and quickly shifting to another.

TOOLS:
- Telephone Game Topic Cards
- Stop-ability Activity Sheet

INSTRUCTIONS:
1. Cut out Telephone Game Topics Cards.
2. Have your student select three topics or pick three topics at random.
3. When beginning to play this game, the student should be able to preview the topics before the game starts.
4. Place the 3 cards face down on the table and imitate a phone ringing and have them pick up one of the cards.
5. The student is to talk about the topic on the card until the phone (you) "ring" again. It is important to stop a student mid-sentence or mid-thought.
6. The student is to pick up another card when the phone (you) "rings" and begin talking about that topic.
7. Repeat this numerous times so that the student has a chance to answer each "phone" twice.
8. At the end, give your student 2 minutes to complete any unfinished stories/thoughts.

INSTRUCTOR TIPS:
- Help students understand that you are not interrupting them to be rude, but to practice shifting quickly between topics.
- Tell your student that they will have 2 minutes at the end of the game to tell you anything they were unable to finish telling you in the game, so that they know they'll have time to finish their thoughts at the end.
- Help students understand the connection between The Telephone Game and real-life by doing the Stop-ability Activity Sheet.
- Have a graphic of a Stop Sign that is a visual reminder for students of the Stop-ability that they've practiced in this game. It can be used anytime you want a student to be able to stop themselves.

www.KandMCenter.com

Copyright ©2012 The K&M Center, Inc.

Stop-Ability

Telephone Game

Topic Cards

School	Food
Best Friend	Sports
Your Favorite Holiday	Pets
Vacations	Family

www.KandMCenter.com

Copyright ©2012 The K&M Center, Inc.

Stop-Ability

Telephone Game

Topic Cards

I love my...	TV Shows
Super Heroes	Fun!
Movies	Beach
I am reading...	In math we are learning...

www.KandMCenter.com

Copyright ©2012 The K&M Center, Inc.

Stop-Ability

Telephone Game

Topic Cards

A place I want to visit	In science I am learning about…
Music	Technology
What's good for our planet?	Exercising
A math fact	Lunchtime is…

www.KandMCenter.com

Copyright ©2012 The K&M Center, Inc.

Stop-Ability

Telephone Game

Topic Cards

www.KandMCenter.com

Copyright ©2012 The K&M Center, Inc.

Spot It

OBJECTIVE:
Race to match symbols on cards in a variety of ways.

TOOLS:
- Spot It Cards (www.kandmcenter.com/the_store/index.cfm?fuseaction=product.display&product_ID=8)

INSTRUCTIONS:
1. Follow the instructions in the Spot It deck. There are a variety of different versions of the game that can be played.

INSTRUCTOR TIPS:
- Encourage students to look by color (red, black, purple, blue, orange) to find the matching image.
- Remind students that matching pictures might be different sizes.
- Try mixing it up by calling the symbols by different names (dinosaur→ T-Rex, ghost→paranormal)

www.KandMCenter.com

Additional Resources

To Support Flexible Thinking

	Optical Illusions
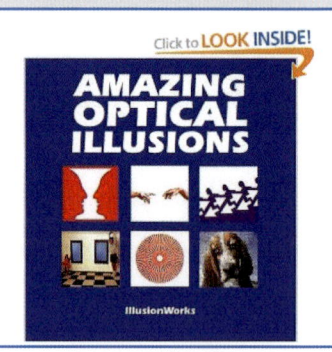	Amazing Optical Illusions by Al Seckel
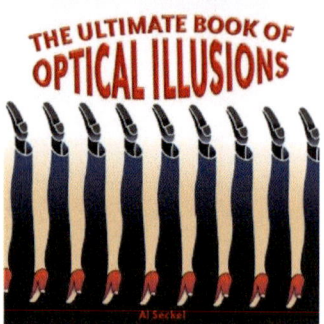	The Ultimate Book of Optical Illusions by Al Seckel
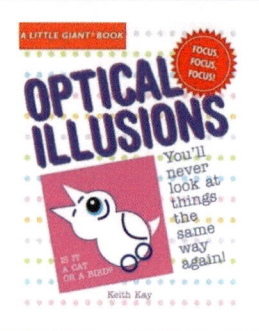	Optical Illusions by Keith Kay
	"Can You Believe Your Eyes?" Card Deck available at www.teachersource.com

www.KandMCenter.com

Copyright ©2012 The K&M Center, Inc.

Additional Games

To Support Flexible Thinking

Games, like the ones embedded in the Flexible Thinking Program, are great venues for encouraging flexible thinking. Here are some more games that encourage flexible thinking and that are a great addition to the Program. Remember, your child should be kept in their Zone of Proximal Development, asked many metacognitive questions, and encouraged to think in new ways. Most importantly, though, have fun!
Ordering information for the games below can be found here :
http://www.kandmcenter.com/the_store/index.cfm?fuseaction=product.display&product_ID=8

Q-Bitz-

This game builds visual dexterity and speed!

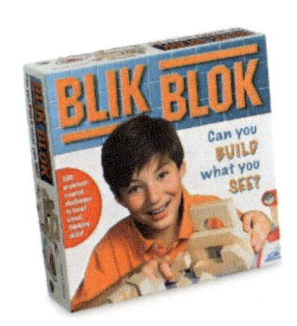

Blik Blok-

Improves 3-D thinking and visual imagine skills, which are important for math, writing and reading comprehension. The ability to mentally rotate and "see" how the pieces go together develops the internal visualization skills used to imagine how to create and develop novel ideas.

Gobblet –

A hyped up tic-tac-toe game. The goal is the same as tic-tac-toe, to get four in a row, or three in a row on Gobblet Jr. The twist is that you have 4 (or 3) sizes of pieces that can "gobble" up another piece smaller than it. This game is quick to start playing, but your skills can continue to develop as you discover more strategies to win. Gobblet Jr. is best for 10 year olds and under. Gobblet is a game everyone can have fun playing.

www.KandMCenter.com

Copyright ©2012 The K&M Center, Inc.

Mastermind-

Code-cracking game. To win quickly, players must use deductive reasoning skills.

Rush Hour-

Wonderful one-person game. The goal is to get the red car out of the traffic jam. Cards increase in difficulty.

Connect Four-

A classic game of vertical checkers. Players are constantly forced to adjust their strategies based on their opponents skill.

Labyrinth-

The constantly changing mazes challenge players to reevaluate their plan after every move.

www.KandMCenter.com

Copyright ©2012 The K&M Center, Inc.

Othello-

The outcome of this game can change at the last minute. Othello rewards players who can think ahead and gain access to key positions on the board.

Additional K&M Learning Products-

Please visit our Store for more games and learning programs!

http://www.kandmcenter.com/the_store/

www.KandMCenter.com

Copyright ©2012 The K&M Center, Inc.

Printed in Great Britain
by Amazon.co.uk, Ltd.,
Marston Gate.